*From the experts who gave us*
*"LinkedIn 101*
*How to Use LinkedIn & Get Connected!"*

# THE
# PERFECT
# RESUME

## Resume 101:
### I'll Show You - How to Write Your
### Best Resume with *Resume Assistant*
### Fueled by LinkedIn

## MICHELLE WEATHERSBY, CQIA,
## PCLC

The Perfect Resume: Resume 101 - I'll Show You - How to Write Your Best Resume with *Resume Assistant* Fueled by LinkedIn

Names: Weathersby, Michelle., author
Title: LinkedIn 101: How to Use LinkedIn & Get Connected!
Description: 1st edition. | Raleigh, NC: Michelle Weathersby Enterprises, [2020]
Identifiers: ISBN- 978-1-953175-03-8
Subjects: Business, Career Development, Leadership

# The Perfect Resume: Resume Writing 101

# I'll Show You - How to Write Your Best Resume with Resume Assistant Fueled by LinkedIn

## Michelle Weathersby, CQIA, PCLC

# Table of Contents

# Introduction

The perfect resume always starts with you with the gifts and talents you have been blessed and born with to help others.

Just imagine…if money were not an issue, what job would you have? How would you use what you have skilled in helping others?

We were made to collaborate with others, so we are interviewing the interviewer to ask technical questions to see if we have the required skill set to accomplish the needed job. Don't worry if you do not fit the job description; maybe it is just a certification away or just a couple of YouTube videos.

Why do I teach this stuff? Because I come across great people with exceptional talents, who do not have the right sales pitch or sales detail sheet about their experience. After seeing SO many people struggle to show their AWESOMENESS, it was important for this book to be written to give a great head start.

## How to use this book

This book is for people with amazing gifts and talents and looking to fuel their career goals. Once you are done with this book, you will have a resume that displays your skills and abilities. You will be locked and ready to go into the fantastic world of resume submission.

## Who needs this book?

Is everyone ready to step up their game and go to the next level of success? If you have had issues expressing who you are and what you can do for an organization when you are a part of their culture? We hear a lot of how NOT to brag about ourselves – this not the book. BRAG, BRAG away. Let your resume show how you can change a department or business with your presence and skill set. Let's dig in.

# Chapter1: The What's & Why's of a Resume

Let's get started. Don't worry, I have been exactly where you are. Not knowing where to go and feeling COMPLETELY overwhelmed by all the choices, verbiage, and formatting.

### *What is a resume?*

It is a formal document that highlights your strengths, successful projects accomplished, leadership skills, community service, and educational qualifications.

It can also let the reader know what you aspire to do.

Next, a resume is a road map of your working life and sometimes your hobbies. Think of all the positions you have held, paid, and unpaid. These all can create open doors for your growth.

A resume is a non-verbal sales pitch or sticker price. How many people do you know who would purchase a car or truck without knowing the facts from a car dealership? You have to be like that salesperson and give the great benefits of this vehicle.

The reader will determine if what you have provided will fit a current need and see if there is a future for your skillset for the department or organization.

## *Why is a great resume needed?*

Simply because it allows recruiters and future employers to quickly know who you are and what you are all about that will lead to employment opportunities, joint ventures, and connecting with key leaders and influencers. It also makes you stand out from the others who may not be willing to invest in their future.

Having that in an organized fashion will allow them to acquire that information in a short period of time.

Let's Get FUELED for an outstanding resume!!!

# Chapter 2: How Do You Get the Perfect Resume?

Just think about what you like to do and what you are good at. Are you currently doing that right now or moving in that direction?

Many careers and jobs are out there, and sometimes we can get caught into a position that we are not enjoying.

A great example is that if you want to be a doctor. Doctors must complete a 4-year undergraduate program, along with **4 years** in medical school and **3** to **7 years** in a residency program to learn the specialty they chose to pursue. And this may be extended longer based on a particular facility.

They have to take Biology, Chemistry, physics, and so many other courses, but this is no big deal for doctors because they knew they wanted to do this.

When I was growing up, I wanted to be a nurse. I am a compassionate person, and I love people. I enjoyed science and chemistry, but I had one big problem.....I would just about faint over blood and large trauma accidents. I would also get queasy when people would get sick around me. Haha, needless to say, that didn't work out.

So, the perfect resume includes your soft and technical skills; both are equally important. Be honest in what you put down and highlight **the relevant information**.

You may be thinking, is that it? Yes, that is it. Your resume's information is always changing as you grow in school, professional positions, and community service.

There is no **"1"** right format, so it is essential to read what the job description is requesting to ensure you cover all the bases.

# Chapter 3: What Is Resume Assistant

In 2016 Microsoft acquired LinkedIn [1] , allowing them to keep their branding and a lot of their functionality to operate on LinkedIn's platform. With this change came, Resume Assistant. It is located on the Microsoft Word application.

Once Microsoft Word is up, we can get started. If you do not have a resume or just need to reformat your current resume, one of the easiest ways is to go to the templates that Word will have in its programming.

### *Newly Created Resume*

If you do not have a resume or need to update your document format, then starting on this page will allow you to search on resume formatting that you may find as a great start.

Finding the right format is important, so start in the search bar and type in resume. This will allow you to see different templates that are available for your use. A

---

[1] https://news.microsoft.com/2016/06/13/microsoft-to-acquire-linkedin/#:~:text=%E2%80%94%20June%2013%2C%202016%20%E2%80%94%20Microsoft,inclusive%20of%20LinkedIn's%20net%20cash.

rule of thumb is to keep it simple if you are not going to email the resume directly to someone.

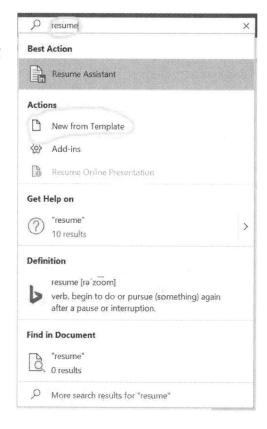

If the format is too fancy, then the automated platform that intakes the resume may be unable to read all of your information, which may take you out as a viable candidate.

As you view the formats available, you are given options that are currently in Word, along with other Microsoft applications that may have something similar to a resume layout or something associated with career development.

Many options are provided, so pick the one that you are most comfortable with revising. Be sure the template you select is not distracting due to:

- Color

- Graphics/Pictures
- Font Size
- Tables/Charts

If different resume templates do not pop up, then select "Resumes and Cover Letters."

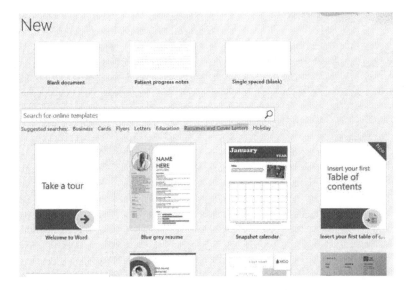

After deciding on the format, select create so you can start updating the information.

## *Revising a Resume*

If you already have a resume, you can pull it up, and most of the time, this screen will pop up on the right of the screen, allowing for immediate usage.

If that does not happen, then on the above toolbar, you will need to select:

- Review
- Then to your right select Resume Assistant to begin engaging

Once your document is up in the "Role" of the application, type in the title of the job you are interested in pursuing. You can also type in the industry you are interested in, which will help you narrow your search. Once you begin typing suggestions for either field, you will pop up to help with the correct verbiage you are seeking.

Resume Assistant pulls information from LinkedIn profiles with similar titles to show you what verbiage has been used by other users who have accounts on LinkedIn.

The information that is provided is:

- Title
- Year
- Description

This information allows you to have an idea of how much experience/responsibility a person had to acquire the duties and goals they had to accomplish.

We will use one of my resume samples throughout the book to refer to.

If you are not getting the results that you wanted, you can either:

**MICHELLE WEATHERSBY**
Raleigh, NC 27601 | 919.601.9033 | michelle.weathersby@lensconsultingfirm.com
in/michelle-weathersby-leadership-executive-career-diversity-training/

### SENIOR-LEVEL MANAGEMENT LEADER – DIVERSITY, EQUITY, INCLUSION ADVISOR

Senior leader who leverages, develops, and maintains effective diverse business relationships at all levels of an organization and business in the community. Demonstrated strategic planning, execution, and evaluation skills for accountability and achieving results. Ability to manage a complex set of stakeholders and advocate change through influence rather than authority by developing and mentoring people and the ability to inspire teams and affect greatness in others through collaboration in a variety of highly competitive industries to contribute to the successful oversight and governance of an organization for small to **Fortune 500 companies.**

> **Industry Knowledge – 20+ years** of experience in diversity & inclusion, operations & information technology industry demonstrating effectiveness through **ROI analysis** and human capital analytics.

> **Business Process Management** – Skilled to review a situation or complex issue from the provided resources and produce effective and efficient viable processes and procedures through senior & executive management while engaging and partnering with the HR team to ensure strategy and business alignment.

> **HR, Learning & Development**– Senior manager with the ability to devise and prepare for possible future events and be equipped for unknown factors using create delivery methods based on audience, capacity, budget, and learning needs. Inspire followership by modeling humility, acting with integrity and fostering inclusion in all facets of work.

*Leadership Highlights*

- Change Management
- Relationship Building
- Strategic Growth
- Coaching & Mentoring
- Organizational Development
- Talent Management
- Succession Planning
- Team Building
- Public Speaking
- Leadership Development
- Training
- Cross-functional Team Leadership
- Project Management
- Human Resources
- Diversity, Equity, Inclusion

### PROFESSIONAL EXPERIENCE

LENS Career – Raleigh, NC *HR Services*                                                                 2007-present
**Senior-Level Management & Advisor**
Develops a strategic plan to advance a firm's mission and objectives and to promote revenue, profitability, and growth as an organization through **leadership, belonging, accessibility, equity justice, diversity & inclusion.** Represent and oversee assigned Learning and Development programs that are implemented in the organization to close business and performance gaps. Ensuring that programs run efficiently and that corporate vision and business needs are both implemented into effective training and leadership programs.

- Work **collaboratively with functional and business process group leaders, operational vice-chairs, business resource group leaders**, diversity champions and ambassadors, and external constituencies to promote and support the implementation and evaluation of best practices related to career growth, diversity and inclusion through creating and implementing senior management development programs.
- Develops the firm's strategic and operational plans while facilitating and implementing these efforts across the firm by managing relationships with partners/vendors.
- Facilitates the embedding of **DEIA perspectives and practices** so that leaders/departments have ownership and investment in the work and designing development of new and existing learning and performance improvement programs.
- Collaborate with Marketing to establish and implement a strategic branding plan to strengthen program awareness and employment value proposition.
- Establish policies that promote company culture, vision and develop a global sourcing strategy and drive the implementation of programs and practices that will attract, develop, and retain a diverse workforce as well as foster an environment of inclusion across the organization.
- Identifies appropriate solutions that satisfy the appropriate business need through classroom & virtual activities.

- Enter another job title in the "Role" field

- Enter another description in the "Industry" field, or

- Select the "Filter examples by top skills" down arrow

This will allow you to review what are some other names that people use with skills similar to yours. Also, you may have to generalize the job title to get larger results.

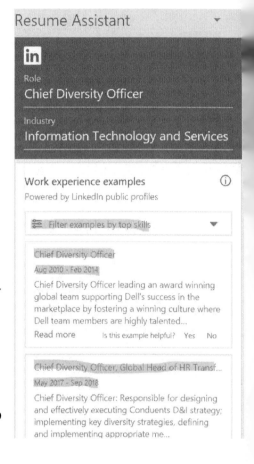

At first, it may seem overwhelming, so you may have to filter the results to narrow down the results.

Select "Filter examples by top skills" will allow you to achieve that.

As you read the examples, give you can use similar verbiage and information as long it pertains to what you have accomplished in your positions.

If you like what is being provided in the job descriptions, your next

step will select the "Read more" to see the complete information.

**Notice:** *The organization's name is not provided, which allows for discretion.*

LinkedIn is always trying to improve its services, so under each job description provided, they were helpful for the completion of your tasks. You do not have to answer this to use the information, but it may help them with providing better communication in the future.

If you still are not satisfied with the descriptions that were provided or needed more information, then you can select the button below to bring you to more examples.

Once you have completed the options provided, then you can press the "Back" to return to your previous results.

See more examples

**Top Skills** - In the next section, you can view some of the topmost used words that people use in your industry to help resume tracking for potential employers.

← Back

Resume Assistant feedback

1. How satisfied are you with Resume Assistant?

1     2     3     4     5
○ —— ○ —— ○ —— ○ —— ○
Not satisfied          Very satisfied

2. Why did you choose that answer? (optional)

⌃
⌄

0/500

3. Anything you would like to add? (optional)

⌃
⌄

0/500

Send Feedback

This verbiage can be used throughout your resume, or you can create a section like the above resume in the "Leadership Highlight" section.

**Give Feedback –** LinkedIn is always trying to optimize their services to reach out to their customers to ensure that they are getting the best service provided.

The answers given will allow the company to receive real concerns to make necessary updates.

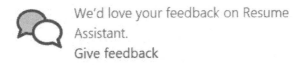

We'd love your feedback on Resume Assistant.
Give feedback

Once the survey is completed, you can select the "Back" to get back to your previous results.

**Articles** – These articles are written by career development experts that can give you further insight into questions you may have about resume writing.

Pressing the article of interest will take you directly to that article; if you select "See more articles on LinkedIn," it will take you to your positing/article page on LinkedIn.

*Note: If you do not have a LinkedIn account, then it will prompt you to create one.*

If you are unsure how to create a great profile, then check out my other book listed on Amazon to create a stellar LinkedIn profile LinkedIn 101: How to Use LinkedIn and Get Connected! Or reach out to me for a one-on-one consultation to get your profile to be an All-Star.

## abc √

This will check your information to ensure that it has a professional tone to it. This can also be accomplished using Grammarly and other similar programs.

## Suggested jobs

The next section gives you listings of jobs that matched the description you put into "Role" and "Industry." You can view the job and apply it to the posting company's website.

This feature portrays many other job boards that allow you to view and apply for the job in different regions.

This is a beneficial insight to let you know that national companies are looking for your particular skill set.

If you are interested in applying for this position, then you can click the "View job on LinkedIn" to use. If you do not have an account, then LinkedIn will prompt you to create a FREE profile account.

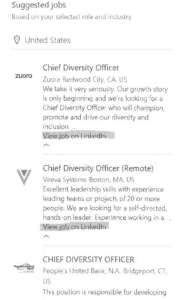

Suggested jobs
Based on your selected role and industry

⊙ United States

**Chief Diversity Officer**
zuora  Zuora Redwood City, CA, US
We take it very seriously. Our growth story is only beginning and we're looking for a Chief Diversity Officer who will champion, promote and drive our diversity and inclusion ...
View job on LinkedIn
∧

**Chief Diversity Officer (Remote)**
Veeva Systems Boston, MA, US
Excellent leadership skills with experience leading teams or projects of 20 or more people. We are looking for a self-directed, hands-on leader. Experience working in a . .
View job on LinkedIn
∧

**CHIEF DIVERSITY OFFICER**
People's United Bank, N.A. Bridgeport, CT, US
This position is responsible for developing

If you are new to the application platform, then you can sign up to be a member, which is free.

If you are a member already, then sign in.

If you do not have the capacity or expertise to start or complete a resume, then keep reading, and let's get your resume right or connect with me at **lensconsultingfirm.com**.

Sometimes the jobs suggested by the Resume Assistant may not be exactly what you are looking for to help to build your resume out. If that is the case, then select "See more jobs on LinkedIn"

See more jobs on LinkedIn  →

Lastly, a fast way to let recruiters know that you are looking for a job transition then select the "Get started on LinkedIn."

This will allow you to select an option in your LinkedIn profile that you are open for recruiters to reach out to you on the platform on jobs that match your skillset.

Let recruiters know you're open

Share that you are open to new opportunities and let your next job find you on LinkedIn

Get started on LinkedIn  →

Just remember that the LinkedIn™ platform is an opportunity to meet and connect with "professional" individuals who could help you to reach your goals. These connections may not be previous friends, co-workers, or associates. Be prepared to reach out to someone you are not familiar with or unfamiliar with you. This is a time to see how each of you can benefit each other to help to go to the next level.

Don't forget to connect with me on LinkedIn.

If you are not sure how to create a stellar LinkedIn profile, then order my book **LinkedIn™ 101: How to Use LinkedIn™ and Get Connected!** Or reach out to me for a one-on-one consultation to get your profile to be an All-Star.

Let's get that ☆**ALL-STAR**☆ status.

# Chapter 4: The Substance

If you start from scratch or already have a document, keep in mind the points listed below. Your resume has to be appealing to the human eye and still skilled enough to get through the automated system known as the Application Tracking System or ATS.

The purpose of using the automated system allows for managers and recruiters to only reach out to individuals who most closely fit the job description listed.

Granted, the more senior-level and executive-level position you are in, you will not have to be concerned with automation. You can add specialized bullets, charts, graphs, and pictures since your resume will be usually given directly to a person.

If you are unsure if your document is going through a system, it would be best to keep the formatting simple.

**Format**
- Maintain plenty of white space.
- Avoid scripts or special symbols

- o Use bullet points for ease of reading and ones that will get through the ATS. Examples:
    - Do: • o ■ · *
    - Don't: ◊ ⚜ ❖
- Select a clear, easy to read font—a few samples.
    - o Do:
        - Time New Romans
        - Cambria
        - Tahoma
        - Garamond
        - Arial
    - o Don't:
        - Algerian
        - Script MT Bold

- Use **bold** or *italic* to draw the reader's eye to key points.
    - o Tone & Structure
    - o Keep your information professional.
    - o Stay positive in what you are conveying, showing that you are an asset to the company.

*\*\*Remember, this is the first impression that is presented about how you conduct business.*

There are necessary items that are needed in a resume. A potential employer or recruiter needs to know these things about you to consider if you can do the job and how to get a hold of you. They are:

- Name & Title (if applicable)
- Contact Information
    - City, State, Zip Code
    - Cell/Telephone Number
    - Email address
    - Website or/and LinkedIn URL
- Summary Statement
- Skill Set (Technical or Soft Skills)
- Professional Experience
- Education
- Volunteer Experience/Community Engagement (optional if there is no room on the resume).

## Name

Recruiters need to know whom they are speaking to. If you are of a specific trade or professional field within medicine, technology, or education, it is important to have that in your title.

## *Example:*

- ✓ Kelly Evans, MD, MSc
- ✓ Sam Jones, SHRM-SCP, MBA-HR
- ✓ Stephen Smith, PCLC

## Contact Information

It is important to have the correct information listed on your resume, so when a company is interested in your experience, you want to make sure that your information is updated and relevant to your position that you are seeking. The formatting is flexible on how it is stated on the document – just make sure it is updated.

## *Examples:*

Kelly Evans, MD, MSc | Denver, CO 56476
312-555-5555 | keyevans@gmail.com
/in/lkellyeva/


Stephen Keller, PMP
Dallas, TX 87360 | 879.904.9878
Stephen.keller@outlook.com
/in/stephen-keller-leadership-training/

## Title & Heading

This section helps to guide and inform the reader what your job position is or what you are looking for. Directing the reader allows for a smoother conversation when you are going through career transitions. A few examples are listed below:

### *Examples:*

✓ HRIS SPECIALIST
Designing Robust Next-Generation Solutions to Meet the HR Needs of Global Manufacturing Organizations

✓ DATABASE MANAGER
Consumer Goods | Pharmaceutical | Health Care Startup Ventures | Turnaround Companies | High-Growth Corporations

✓ Objective: Principal Training & Development Professional

✓ *Targeted position:* Director of Customer Success & Strategy

✓ Storyteller | Youth Advocate | Program Manager Strategist

✓ Life & Family Coach | Keynote Speaker | Microsoft Suite Guru

- ✓ Marketing Specialist | Social Media Consultant | Event Program Manager
- ✓ IT Specialist | Cyber Security Advisor | Networking Facilitator
- ✓ Senior Program/Project Manager | Clinical Trial Auditor | Business Administrator

## Summary

A lot of us have so much experience that we want the recruiter or hiring manager to know all of our accomplishments. The problem is that there is not enough time for the person who is reviewing resumes to look at anyone's entire work history in detail without it starts to become a full-time job.

The summary allows for you to briefly inform the recruiter or manager what you are, what you have done, and what you can do for your future employer.

### *Examples:*

- ✓ **Human Resources Professional** with 5+ years' experience building and leading best-in-class HR organizations for major corporations in the technology industry. Expertise includes technical staff and management recruitment, onboarding, training and development, employee relations, performance standards and evaluation metrics, and

HRIS technology. Collaborate with diverse multinational teams globally to leverage human capital to meet challenging business needs.

✓ Strategic and innovative analyst who translates business vision into initiatives that **improve performance, profitability, growth**, and employee engagement. Empowering leader who supports companies and management with a unique perspective and appreciation for the organization's growth. Genuine influencer who thrives on tough challenges and translates visions and strategies into actionable, value-added goals.

✓ Dynamic, versatile **Bilingual Executive Office Administrator with 15+ years** of experience, providing administrative support to foreign diplomats, office management, human resources and vendor management that thrives in a demanding, fast-paced environment. Proven leader with the ability to multi-task while remaining positive and productive with changing priorities displaying continued attention to detail. Innovative, confident, and poised, possessing strong problem-solving skills, and able to anticipate needs and proactively address issues, while establishing and maintaining working relationships with staff across all levels.

✓ Self-motivated professional with **experience in developing a professional rapport with clients to perform clinical assessments, diagnosis, and development of treatment plans** to support the whole client using a strength-based approach. Knowledge in writing comprehensive clinical assessments, personal centered plans, and service plans. Experience working with a multidisciplinary team to ensure clients receive continuity of care.

Ability to provide trauma informed services. Proficient in social work code of ethics, and case management standards. Knowledge of government programs and community resources. Skilled in assisting with life skills, personal financial planning, and budgeting.

✓ ***Promoting optimal performance, reliability, and security across core business systems by being*** exceptionally skilled and resourceful **IT Risk & Security Specialist** with strong attention to detail and excellent customer service. Highly adept at bringing multiple simultaneous projects to completion by or before strict deadlines. Superb skills in explaining complex technical concepts to a variety of professional and non-professional audiences.

## Skills – Technical or Soft

A listing of skills of what you can do allows the document reader to scan the list briefly to see if the skills requested and others are beneficial to the requested role. This can be technical skills in nature that are directed for that particular industry; it could be a list of soft/technical skills that are transferrable between industries, or it could be a little bit of both.

This type of information will allow the reader to see what you are currently are capable of and how your skill will be integrated into the department or organization.

Starting off with 6-8 skills is a good beginning. This should be displayed in 2 to 3 columns for ease of reading. And remember, this section should not cover half the page.

✓ SALES

- B2B Sales Growth
- Financial and Business Process Management
- Customer Service & Satisfaction
- Operations Management
- Client Service Management

- Business Development
- Product Training and Placement
- Strategic Account Development
- Strong Communicator
- Sales & Marketing

✓ LEGAL

- Attorney
- Associate
- Litigator
- Paralegal
- Adjudication
- Affidavits

- Briefs
- Case Law
- Client Management
- Conflict Resolution

✓ NURSING

- Assessment
- BSN
- Care
- Case
- Clinical

- Communicate
- Compassion
- Health
- License

**Professional Experience**

This is more of a breakdown of what you have done for each job you may have done within your entire job history or what is relevant for the position that you are applying for.

**Example**: If you are applying for a technology position, there is no need for you to list your role as a shoe salesperson that you had done before unless it leaves a huge gap in your work history.

If you do need to include this information, then try to only add the transferrable duties you had for the posted position.

Adding irrelevant information can easily take you out of running for a job because the ATS will pull this information, skewing the company's algorithm for finding the right candidate.

Also, having this information, your resume will begin to have recruiters contacting you for jobs you are not interested in going back to or has no relevance to your goals.

## Education

Listing this information alerts the reader where you received your degrees, certifications, and training and see if it is relevant for the posted position. This section also allows them to know that you are open to improving yourself and growing.

If you have not completed a degree or training, then listing the relevant classes and anticipated year of completion will help the reader see how far you may be along in the program.

Something is better is nothing. You do not have to have a degree to be successful in certain industries but it is important to the reader that you taking continued classes to improve your knowledge and staying abreast of the industry changes.

- ✓ **Bachelor of Arts (B.A.)**, University of Hartford - Hartt School of Music BM Music Management & Vocal Performance | West Hartford, CT

- ✓ **Business of Administration, certification**, Barney School of Business General Studies | Massachusetts, CT *courses: Financial Management, Managerial Accounting, Micro & Macro Economics*

✓ **Languages:** German (Fluent), Dutch (Conversational), French & Italian (Basic)

✓ *Executive MBA,* TEXAS A&M UNIVERSITY / GPA 4.0

✓ *B.Sc. in Business Management with a concentration in Sales & Marketing,* KAPLAN UNIVERSITY / CUM LAUDE

✓ *Affiliations:* Association of Equipment Management Professionals • National Society of Leadership and Success

✓ *Technical Skills & Training:* GX Developer • GT Developer • Linux/Windows Oss • Construction Equipment Management Program for equipment, operations and financial managers • Sales Training • Service & Customer Satisfaction

## Volunteering/Community Engagement

Don't skip on this section if you can. Many times, people have been invited to interview or even hired because this section was completed.

Even though a high percentage of resumes are first filtered through a system, it still needs to be reviewed by a person. The reviewer may see a common interest that you do and would like to know how you play a part.

Learning how to navigate the correct wording and knowing how to use the most current tools will begin to give you that great advantage for your next opportunity.

## *Examples:*

- ✓ National Blood Foundation Research & Education Trust
  –AABB, WASHINGTON, DC
  Board of Trustees, Governance Committee
  2015-Present

- ✓ Professional Musical Leader & Volunteer • Youth
  Leader • Various Religious Organizations Volunteer

- ✓ **Strategy Advisor** | Hope 4 The Brave - 2008 - Present
  **Youth Advisor** | CKJ College Preparatory School - 2006
  - Present

# Chapter 5: Military to Civilian

First, THANK YOU FOR SERVING!

No matter what position you have had in the military, the language is different on your professional documents versus what is on a civilian's professional documents. The same steps mentioned above should still be used. It is important to know if the wording that is being presented is "corporate speak".

Listed below are some transitional words that can help you move in the right direction. We want to make sure that your responsibilities are adequately reflected.

## *Job Titles*

- Colonel = SVP/EVP/CxO
- Captain = Vice President/CxO
- Commander = Director or Senior Manager
- Executive Officer = Managing Director
- Field Grade Officer = Executive or Manager
- Company Grade Officer = Operations Manager
- Warrant Officer =Technical Specialist or Department Manager
- Senior NCOs = Supervisor
- Infantry = Security Force
- First Sergeant = Manager
- Squad Leader = Team Leader or Supervisor
- Supply Sergeant = Logistics Manager
- Operations NCO= Supervisor

## Manager of People

- Supervisor
- Manager
- Director
- VP/SVP/EVP/CxO

## Manager of Process

- SME (Subject Matter Expert)
- Process Manager
- Principal
- Supervisor

## Duties & Responsibilities

- AI= additionally skilled in
- combat = hazardous conditions
- company = company, department
- medal = award
- military personnel office = human resources
- mission = task/function/objective
- military occupation specialty/classification = career specialty
- squad/platoon = team or department
- reconnaissance = data collection and analysis
- regulations= policy, guidelines, laws
- security clearance= security clearance
- service members = employees, associates
- subordinates = employees, associates
- TAD/TDY = business trip

These changes are significant to make because the keyword scanning function of an ATS can lead hiring managers to you. Some reports indicate that ATS systems are looking for matches of 75% and above. In contrast, other reports suggest that major corporations that receive thousands of resumes every day prefer 80% or above matches.

**\*\*Federal resumes** *should be completed similar to the steps listed above, but the document will need to be very lengthy according to the directions of the job descriptions and guidelines. The document is usually consisting of 3-7 pages.*

# Chapter 6: The Purpose

Sometimes the question is asked why I have to put so much into a resume. We have to remember that this may be the only way to properly get into the door of places where we want to be. Even though word of mouth is a great referral, we can get so busy with business that we forget, and a document with our information can help to bring your qualities to that reader.

The resume is also needed to compare your information against someone else's, and of course, the fastest that way is done is through using scanners of your resume.

Your resume should get straight to the point allowing the reader to quickly scan and pick up what they need within a matter of seconds. Having a document that is over 2-pages can make it a little more difficult for that efficient review.

Using the Resume Assistant allows this process to be simpler with updated information on what your competition is using to the attention of managers, investors, and organizations.

### You Did IT - Almost! Now What?

Wow! That was a LOT! Way to go, but don't stop now! Finish up to make that resume stand out.

Your resume may not entirely be what you want, and I understand. Don't worry, you have done a TREMENDOUS job and headed in the right direction, but now you need to optimize and maximize your resume so the right people find it.

It may be time to reach out to a professional career coach and get help with your professional document. If you reach out to me, this is what will happen when you invest in a session? Let me tell you:

1. I will personally review your resume ahead of time to come up with suggestions, questions, and strategies to help you slay your resume. No rock will be left unturned. We will go over your statement, contact information, header, employment history, education, volunteering, awards, and accomplishments sections, ensuring all are completed and accurate.

2. Coaching: In this part of the session, we will go over the following: who are you, what do you want to accomplish, whom you want to work with, and what do you do?

3. By the time we are done, my team and I will have all the information to update, optimize, and maximize your resume during our time together.

Does that sound JUST like what the Resume doctor ordered? I thought so, and that' why I wanted you to know about it. **Review lensconsultingfirm.com** and see which service best fits your needs.

Reach out today, and let's get connected.

# Conclusion

You are off to a great start and closer to the finish than ever, and I just helped one more person get closer to his/her dreams. It feels incredible, doesn't it? I know it does. I am SO proud of you. Now the journey gets better, don't forget to implement ALL the principles I taught you and watch ALL the hot leads come in.

Presenting your skillset to your current employer or potential employer is always needed when looking to go to the next level.

# Tips & Templates

## #1 - Keep it Simple 1-2 pages

If a hiring manager is spending ten seconds or less looking at your resume, he or she might not get to the 3 or more pages! Remember the purpose of it—it's not to showcase everything you've ever done, but rather to show that you have the background, skills, and experience for the job posted.

*(This may not apply to scientific, entertainment, military/federal, or college entry resumes)*

## #2 – Update Your Information ASAP

One of the easiest ways to stay on top of your resume is to update it within 1-2 months of a new job. This allows you to use the job description provided that was given when you were hired and the actual duties you are performing daily.

## #3 – Remove old information

Technology is moving at breakneck speed. Suppose your resume does not reflect the current changes and relevant application updates. In that case, this can be a signal to a recruiter or hiring manager that you are flexible to changes.

## #4 – Keywords & Right Job Title

Review the job description to ensure that your verbiage and wording match similar language used. This should only take quick tweaking. You can use at least one of the tools below to see if you are reaching the right percentage for keywords.

- https://tagcrowd.com/

- https://www.wordclouds.com/?utm_campaign=el earningindustry.com&utm_source=%2Fthe-8-best-free-word-cloud-creation-tools-for-teachers&utm_medium=link

- https://worditout.com/word-cloud/create

## #5 – Most Information at The Top

Depending on if you are just entering the workforce or updating your resume, you need to put your most relevant and essential information at the top of the document. We want to catch and keep our audience's attention.

## #6 – Use the Word Tools

If you are using Microsoft Word or Google docs, consider utilizing a spellcheck tool that comes with the application or purchases something like Grammarly. We all need a little help. Typos are a bad look.

## #7 – Military to Civilian resume

If you are transitioning from the military to corporate American, it is important to change your resume to reflect corporate "speak."

## #8 – Humans Only

Your resume should show knowledge within your industry, but there is a saying too much of a good thing is not good. Include industry language but don't go overboard.

## #9 – Address the Gaps

Don't be afraid to address the work gaps. Fill them up with what you were doing. This could be:

- Trainings
- Volunteer work

- Writing a book

Whatever it is, make sure it shows that you have been moving forward and growing.

## #10 – Keep It Professional

Remember that this professional document is only for relevant professional information. Personal information may be off-putting to the reader, especially if it has nothing to do with your skillset for the job you are applying for.

# Sample Resumes

## Entry Level – This should only be 1 page

**MARCEY ERSON**

Marketing Associate

### ACADEMIC HISTORY

**QUARKWOOD UNIVERSITY**

Bachelor of Science in Marketing, 2016-2020

- Latin Honors Cum Laude Awardee
- Consistent Dean's Honor Lister
- Outstanding Marketing Student Awardee 2019
- Member of the Entrepreneurship Club

**GOOGLE**

Certification, 2012-2016

- Academic Excellence in English, History, and Mathematics
- President of the Beachtown Business Club
- Staff Member of the Student Government

### PROFESSIONAL PROFILE SUMMARY

I develop, implement and oversee the online marketing strategy for organizations. I create and execute digital marketing campaigns and web content

### SKILLS AND ABILITIES

- Marketing Skills
- Copywriting Skills
- Content Development Skills
- Time Management and Organizational Skills
- Communication and Presentation Skills

### ACHIEVEMENTS

- Received the Excellence in Marketing Award 2022
- Earned the ZimCore Creative Employee of Year 2021
- Featured in Neoxgenera Mag's Top 100 Marketing Moguls

### CAREER HISTORY

**MARKETING ASSOCIATE**

ZimCore Creative Labs, 2021-present

- Conceptualized and executed successful traditional and digital marketing campaigns
- Analyzed market research findings
- Developed marketing calendar

**MARKETING SPECIALIST**

Elklessa Solutions, Co., 2020-2021

- Researched consumer preferences and marketing trends
- Planned and implemented marketing strategies
- Collaborated with the creative and strategy teams

### CONTACT DETAILS:

Phone: 123-456-7890
Email: hello@reallygreatsite.com
LinkedIn: @reallygreatsite
Website: reallygreatsite.com
123 Anywhere St., Any City, State

# Andy Palmer

## JUNIOR ACCOUNTANT

## PROFILE BACKGROUND

Experienced accountant in corporate bookkeeping and financial budgeting. Along with development, implementation and overseeing the online marketing strategy for organizations. by executing digital marketing campaigns and web content.

## ACADEMIC HIGHLIGHTS

**Beekewood University**
BS Accountancy | Graduated in 2013

- Dean's Lister
- Graduated with honors (GPA: 3.87)
- Member, Beekewood Accounting Association
- Awarded the Dean's Citation for Academic Excellence

## CORE SKILLS

- Payroll accounting and tax computation
- Budget forecasting
- Cost analysis and system automation
- Accounts Receivable/Accounts Payable
- Internal auditing

## PROFESSIONAL CAREER

**Senior Accountant**
*Kerkland Associates | 2017-present*

- Prepares asset, liability and capital account entries
- Compiles and analyzes account information
- Documents financial transactions and performs audits

**Junior Accountant**
*Media Masonry, Incorporated | 2013-2017*

- Prepared and examined financial records for the company
- Ensured accuracy of records and timely payment of taxes
- Performed regular internal audits

## CONTACT:

Landline: 123 456 7890
Mobile: +123 456 7890
Address: 123 Anywhere St., Any City, State, Country 12345
Email: hello@reallygreatsite.com
www.reallygreatsite.com

## VOLUNTEER

- Street photography - Boys & Girls Club
- Reading non-fiction - Elementary Students

# Mid Career – 1or 2 pages

HENRI SMITH

Digital Marketer

## MY BACKGROUND

I develop, implement and oversee the online marketing strategy for organizations. I create and execute digital marketing campaigns and web content.

## SPECIALIZATIONS

Digital Marketing
Web Content Creation
Visual Storytelling
Social Media Campaigns
Paid Social Media Advertising
Email Marketing
Search Engine Optimization

## CONTACT INFORMATION

Telephone: 123-456-7890
Email:
hello@reallygreatsite.com
LinkedIn: @reallygreatsite
123 Anywhere St., Any City, State, Country 12345
www.reallygreatsite.com

## CAREER BACKGROUND

### DIGITAL STRATEGIST
Web Kandi Services, Co. | 2017-present
- Develops, implements and manages marketing campaigns for various clients
- Works with graphic designers for web design and digital storytelling

### SOCIAL MEDIA MANAGER
Webby Sabby Digital, Inc. | 2015-2017
- Wrote copy for the website and social media platforms
- Planned and executed social media campaigns
- Measured the effectiveness of said campaigns

## EDUCATION & TRAINING

### LINKEDIN
Certification in Online Marketing & SEO

### UNIVERSITY OF EL DORADO
Bachelor of Arts, Major in Communications

## LEADERSHIP ACHIEVEMENTS

Marketer's Awardee two years in a row
Digital Strategist of the Year, 2017
Regular Speaker at the Marketer's Annual Conference

# GRETA MAE EVANS

PHOTOGRAPHER

## CAREER BACKGROUND

### SENIOR PHOTOGRAPHER

The Flotonic Imaging Studios | 2019-present

- Organized and conducted in-studio and on-location photo shoots
- Managed and monitored the photography team
- Captured high-quality photographs

### PROFESSIONAL PHOTOGRAPHER

Palmllow Photography Studios | 2018-2019

- Shot and produced top-notch photos
- Edited and retouched photos as needed
- Assisted with photo shoot production
- Maintained studio and camera equipment

## ACADEMIC BACKGROUND

### QUARKWOOD UNIVERSITY

Bachelor of Arts in Photography | 2016-2018

- Graduated with Latin Honors, Cum Laude
- Vice President of the Photography and Film Club
- Official Photographer of the student publication, Quarkwood Herald

### WINSHIRE VIDEOGRAPHY PROGRAM

- Secretary of the Photographers Club
- Photographer of the Winshire Wall publication

## PERSONAL INFO

I am a dedicated and self-motivated professional photographer with years of experience in capturing high-quality photos and managing photo shoots.

## SPECIALIZATIONS

- Portrait Photography
- Event Photography
- Wedding Photography
- Street Photography
- Photo Manipulation
- Digital Illustration
- Graphic Design

## LET'S GET IN TOUCH!

Landline: 123-456-7890
Mobile: 123-456 7890
Email: hello@reallygreatsite.com
Portfolio: www.reallygreatsite.com
Studio: 123 Anywhere Street, Any City, State

## SKILLS AND ABILITIES

- Knowledge of Camera Equipment Usage and Photo Editing Softwares
- Interpersonal Skills
- Time Management and Organizational Skills
- Artistic Ability

# Director/Principal Level – 1 or 2 pages

# JASONMARTIN
## Director of Design & Strategy

My Name Is Jason Martin lorem empus id fringilla molestie ornare diam in olestie ipsum etium rosn ollicitudin est, porttitor amet hitmassa Done cporttitor dolor shit dolor kiren lorem nisl molestie pretium etfring. is the shitp lorem ipcum retiumci amet is tudinest.moles tium lorem olestie pretium apaza all the rosen. fringilla lorem ipsum .

### EXPERIENCE

**Lead Web Designer**
2015 - 2017

SOFT DESIGN STUDIOS

Porttitor amet massa Done cporttitor dolor et nisl molestie ium feliscon lore ipsum dolor tfringilla, lorem lorem ipsum. ollcitudin est dolor time.

**Senior Web Designer**
2013 - 2015

WEB TECH LTD

Porttitor amet massa Done cporttitor dolor et nisl molestie ium feliscon lore ipsum dolor tfringilla, lorem lorem ipsum. ollcitudin est dolor time. Done cporttitor

**Lead Web Designer**
2010 - 2013

DEV CREATIVE SOLUTION

Porttitor amet massa Done cporttitor dolor et nisl molestie ium feliscon lore ipsum dolor tfringilla, lorem lorem ipsum. ollcitudin.

**Senior Web Designer**
2008 - 2010

DEV CREATIVE SOLUTION

Porttitor amet massa Done cporttitor dolor et nisl molestie ium feliscon lore ipsum dolor tfringilla, lorem lorem ipsum. ollcitudin.

008 659 864 4568

www.jasonmartin.com

jasonmartin123@mail.com

## PERSONAL

| | |
|---|---|
| Birthday | 12th January 1991 |
| Relationship | Single |
| Nationality | Egyptian |
| Languages | English, Arabic |

## SKILLS

Communication
Creativity
Teamwork
Organizational
Leadership
Teamplayer

## SOFTWARE

PHOTOSHOP
ILLUSTRATOR
INDESIGN
MS OFFICE
HTML 5
CSS

### EDUCATION

**Name of university**
2010 - 2013

CERTIFICATE OF WEB TRAINIG

Porttitor amet massa Done cporttitor dolor et nisl molestie ium feliscon lore ipsum dolor tfringilla, lorem lorem ipsum. ollcitudin est dolor time. lorem ipsum.

**Name of university**
2007 - 2009

BECHELOR OF ART DIRECTOR

Porttitor amet massa Done cporttitor dolor et nisl molestie ium feliscon lore ipsum dolor tfringilla, lorem lorem ipsum. ollcitudin est dolor time.

**Name of university**
2007 - 2009

HIGHER SECENDERY EXAMINITION

Porttitor amet massa Done cporttitor dolor et nisl molestie ium feliscon lore ipsum dolor tfringilla, lorem lorem ipsum. ollcitudin est dolor time.

## CONTACT ME

**Addres**
126, Street mahon,
New York City, USA

**Phone**
0123 4567 8910 1230
0123 4567 8910 1230

**Web**
contact@email.com
www.ownsite.com

## PRO SKILLS

PHOTOSHOP

ILLUSTRATOR

INDESIGN

MS WORD

MS EXCEL

## FOLLOW ME

**Facebook**
facebook.com/yourname

**linkedin**
linkedin.com/in/yourname

**Twitter**
twitter.com/yourname

# HENRY MADISON
## ART DIRECTOR

 **EXPERIENCE**

| | |
|---|---|
| **2015 - 2018**<br>**Vison Multitune.net** | SENIOR WEB DEVELOPER<br>Porttitor amet massa Done cporttitor dolor et nisl molestie ium feliscon lore ipsum dolor tfringilla. lorem lorem ipsum. oilcitudin est dolor time. Done cporttitor dolor kiren |
| **2013 - 2015**<br>**Soft Tech Lomited** | LEAD WEB DEVELOPER<br>Porttitor amet massa Done cporttitor dolor et nisl molestie ium feliscon lore ipsum dolor tfringilla. lorem lorem ipsum. oilcitudin est dolor time. Done cporttitor |
| **2011- 2013**<br>**Creative Corporation** | WEB & GRAPHIC DESIGNER<br>Porttitor amet massa Done cporttitor dolor et nisl molestie ium feliscon lore ipsum dolor tfringilla. lorem lorem ipsum. oilcitudin est dolor time. Done cporttitor |

 **EDUCATION**

| | |
|---|---|
| **2010 - 2015**<br>**Asian University** | BACHELORS OF ARTS<br>Porttitor amet massa Done cporttitor dolor et nisl molestie ium feliscon lore ipsum dolor tfringilla. |
| **2008 - 2010**<br>**Creative School** | HIGHER SECONDARY EXAMINATION<br>Porttitor amet massa Done cporttitor dolor et nisl molestie ium feliscon lore ipsum dolor tfringilla. |
| **2006 - 2008**<br>**Creative School** | HIGHER SECONDARY EXAMINATION<br>Porttitor amet massa Done cporttitor dolor et nisl molestie ium feliscon lore ipsum dolor tfringilla. |
| **2004 - 2006**<br>**Creative School** | HIGHER SECONDARY EXAMINATION<br>Porttitor amet massa Done cporttitor dolor et nisl molestie ium feliscon lore ipsum dolor tfringilla. |

 **REFERENCES**

| | |
|---|---|
| **Jonathon Deo**<br>Director<br>Phone: +555 123 5566<br>Email: jonathondeo@gmail.com | **Jabin Smith**<br>Web developer<br>Phone: +123 5556 4455<br>Email: jabinsmith@gmail.com |

# Author Information

The author can be found at:

**LinkedIn:** https://www.linkedin.com/in/michelle-weathersby-leadership-executive-career-diversity-training/

**Facebook:** https://www.facebook.com/LENSConsultingFirm/

**Twitter:** @lenscareer

**Instagram:** lensconsulting

Michelle Weathersby is the CEO of LENS Consulting Firm and Michelle Weathersby Enterprises. She is certified as an Executive Career Life Coach and Quality Improvement Associate/Process Master and degreed in Leadership Studies and Human Resource Management. Through her education and experience, she works with clients by positioning them to receive the career level and financial backing desired by advising them on professional profiles and documents for Personal/Business LinkedIn Profiles, Press Releases, Media Kits, Wikipedia Profiles, Capability Statements & Resumes along with other career development services.

Michelle enjoys helping individuals and organizations leverage their skills and talents to achieve their desired goals by collaborating with diverse teams of professionals to accomplish new levels of success in various highly competitive industries. One of the main benefits of retaining Michelle's services for non-profits to large Fortune 100 & 500 companies is the successful attainment of an organization's human capital.

Michelle also partners with leading national professional organizations to provide overall service for growth and success, and she is a Forbes council member contributor writer and a writer for other local magazines about career development.